EXAMPLE
THIS BOOK

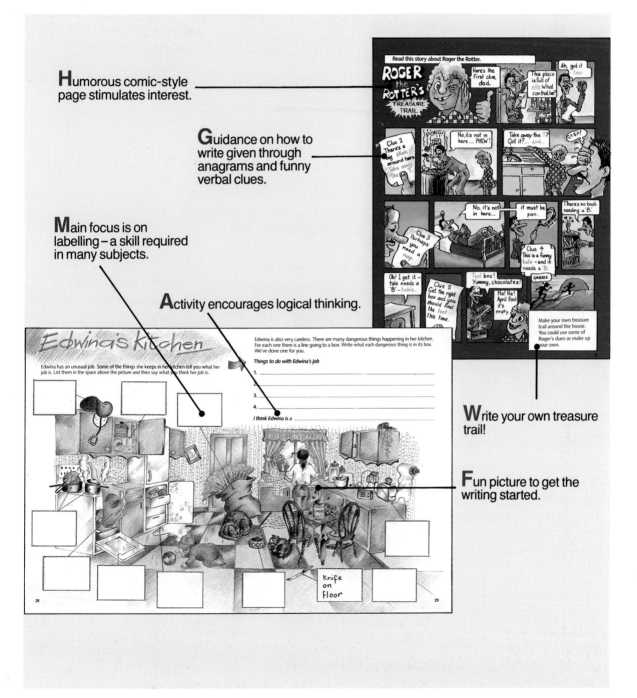

Humorous comic-style page stimulates interest.

Guidance on how to write given through anagrams and funny verbal clues.

Main focus is on labelling – a skill required in many subjects.

Activity encourages logical thinking.

Write your own treasure trail!

Fun picture to get the writing started.

*T*he entire process of writing – for life – has one very practical purpose: communication. All writing is for communication.

In Writing 2, activities are used to develop different types of written communication – writing letters, creative story writing, making lists and notes, writing poems and so on.

As part of these activities, and as separate ones too, we also improve skills in three vital areas.

SPELLING & VOCABULARY

Like illegible handwriting, poor spelling can make a bad impression and make communication difficult.

Reading a wide range of books can help. So will the spelling activities in this book and the Success! Practice books.

But it's also vital to encourage the growth of a rich vocabulary. Give your child the confidence to try out new words – talk about different ways of saying things, and repeat new words once or twice so that they get the hang of them.

Among others these activities will help:

Sid Genius and Tatty Tricia on page 16 contains a number of very common spelling and punctuation errors to spot and correct. Sid Genius gives all the right answers as usual. Can your child find all the errors? Are there any that cause particular problems?

Poems that have shapes on page 19 provides a framework (literally!) for the choice of appropriate vocabulary. The chosen words are put within a shape – a concrete poem is thus written.

A tricky wordsearch on page 22 involves a number of words which are often spelt incorrectly. Attention is drawn to the most common errors, with encouragement to write the words carefully and correctly. This isn't a dreary copying exercise – it's in the form of a wordsearch which most children will enjoy doing.

BOOK

Handwriting

Legible writing is important – your child can't communicate ideas if the writing can't be read. Also neat handwriting tends to get higher marks in exams!

These are some of the activities that will help:

A handwriting riddle on page 8 involves thinking about and describing different handwriting styles. If your child is aware of their own handwriting style this is the first important step towards improvement.

In a dark, dark wood on page 12 requires the copying out of a poem. It has to be done neatly and within given lines. To add interest and a further useful skill, your child is asked to put the lines of the poem in the right order first.

Post a poster on page 40 encourages the use of different styles of lettering in order to create a poster. With its emphasis on neatness and layout this activity will help your child to take a pride in the appearance of their work.

66 GRAMMAR! 99

This is a basic understanding of the way words work together, so it is about parts of speech and grammatical rules, punctuation, sentence construction and so on.

Activities like these encourage thinking about the way our language works. This will make your child's writing better.

The Chartbusters on page 10 involves the selection of appropriate adjectives. The activity is designed to increase awareness of how words function. You could (gently!) draw attention to Sid Genius' comment at the bottom of the page.

In 2020 on page 13 asks for the use of the future tense. Most children get their tenses right when they speak, but they sometimes become confused when they write. If you notice the present tense creeping in here, read what your child has written out loud. They'll probably spot the mistakes.

The cellar on page 20 focuses on the punctuation of speech, which often causes difficulty. The words spoken by characters in a mystery story have to be written out within the correct speech marks – check to see how well your child has done.

HOW THIS BOOK *works*

You can share in the fun of **Success!** If you want, you can do some of the activities with your child. But **Success!** does not depend on you. One of the benefits of the range is to encourage children to enjoy working independently, not just when the grown-ups are around.

YOU

have a special role to play. It's the one that comes naturally to any parent: give all the encouragement you can!

If you can give your child the benefits of more individual attention, there is no need for you to *teach* specific skills. **Success!** does not require specialist knowledge.

WHEN

you're ready to start on this book at home, sit down together and go through it. Talk about the activities and the zany characters, and enjoy the often crazy situations. Start one or two activities to get the feel of them.

Then, help to choose an activity to be completed and say that you'd like to see it when it's done.

HOW

will you know things are going well? When your child is absorbed, *thinking* about the activity and really *doing* the work, then you'll know that progress is being made. Look at the back of this book for further guidance.

Speed isn't important. Enjoyment and commitment are the telling signs.

WHAT

should your response be? Praise the results – don't criticise. If you think there

is a better way of doing something, suggest it as an alternative, not as the only right way.

Make it clear that working at the activities is a good thing which brings praise. Effort does deserve recognition and it *will* bring results. Not least important, it will give confidence and increase enthusiasm for more activities and more learning.

Look out for opportunities to encourage work on other activities but go for short, frequent sessions – don't let it get boring!

Don't forget to *tick* off each completed activity on the *contents* page and share the sense of achievement and pleasure.

Success! contents

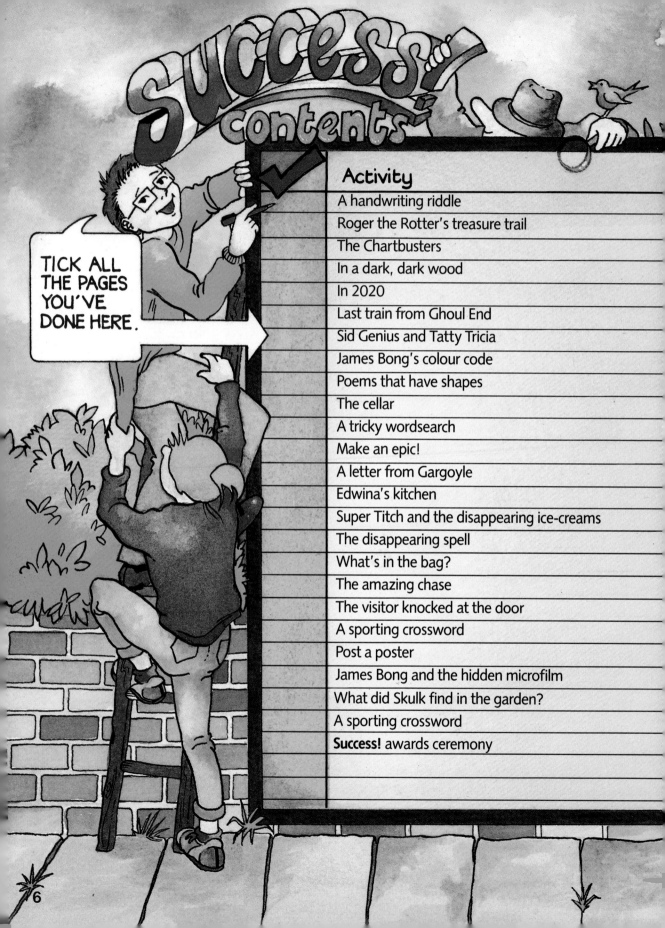

> TICK ALL THE PAGES YOU'VE DONE HERE.

	Activity
	A handwriting riddle
	Roger the Rotter's treasure trail
	The Chartbusters
	In a dark, dark wood
	In 2020
	Last train from Ghoul End
	Sid Genius and Tatty Tricia
	James Bong's colour code
	Poems that have shapes
	The cellar
	A tricky wordsearch
	Make an epic!
	A letter from Gargoyle
	Edwina's kitchen
	Super Titch and the disappearing ice-creams
	The disappearing spell
	What's in the bag?
	The amazing chase
	The visitor knocked at the door
	A sporting crossword
	Post a poster
	James Bong and the hidden microfilm
	What did Skulk find in the garden?
	A sporting crossword
	Success! awards ceremony

A handwriting riddle

Can you match the handwriting to the people?

My writing is curly and neat.

A packet of tea
A pound of butter

My writing is tiny, spidery and wobbly.

Dear Mary,
Thankyou for your letter.
I did enjoy reading it.

Uncle John

My writing is thin and tall and scrawly.

I think mice are nice.
I think mice are...

Handwriting can be

scrawly   curly   easy to read   tidy   difficult to read   untidy

huge   tall   spidery

tiny   wobbly   thin

neat   small

Grandad

Gran

What is Sid Genius' writing like?

writing which is easy to read is legible - writing which is difficult to read is illegible

And what about Tatty Tricia's?

And Gargoyle's?

Sid Genius is boring!

Ghouls are great!

What is your handwriting like?

Tell the truth! Fill in the space here.

My writing is...

Read this story about Roger the Rotter.

THE CHARTBUSTERS

This group is booked to appear in your local hall next week. As a reporter for the local paper you have to find out the *real facts* about the group.

You need to think up a good name for the band first.

My name for the band is

I really am excited about meeting fantastic Fred.

Then choose several words from these lists which best describe each member of the band.

Wally **Sid** **Horace** **Fred**

weedy	sleepy	hairy	fantastic
wishy-washy	small	hideous	fat
wet	shaky	hunky	foolish
wonderful	silly	handsome	famous
worn-out	slow	healthy	fearful
weary	smelly	heavenly	flimsy
weird	snoozy	horrible	foul
wheezy	sad	heroic	forgetful
wild	scruffy	huge	freckly
wise	sensible	humble	frightened
wobbly	shaggy	hungry	fuzzy
wrinkled	sickly	happy	fabulous
wicked	selfish	helpless	feeble
wiry	scared	hulky	filthy
	serious		flabby
	short		fierce
			friendly
			funny

Now see if you can write the newspaper article, using some of the words you have chosen. You might want to include these things.

Where is the band to play? On what day? Have you been able to interview any of the band? Where can tickets be bought? How much are they? Will there be a large audience?

In a dark dark wood

SNIP! SNIP!

Oh no, she's cut up the poem! Now it's all in the wrong order!

Can you copy out the poem in the right order? Then can you finish off the poem? Remember to write in the lines.

Make sure the **ascenders** touch the top line. These are the tall letters: b, d, f, h, k, l, t. Make sure the **descenders** touch the bottom line. These are the letters that go below the line: g, j, p, q, y.

In a dark, dark wood

There were some dark, dark stairs

In that dark, dark room

There was a dark, dark cottage

Up those dark, dark stairs

In that dark, dark cottage

There was a dark, dark room

There was a dark, dark

What might you find in the room?

a dark, dark box?

Write it here

In

a dark, dark cupboard?

a dark, dark cab

a dark, dark vase?

What do you find inside?

12

Dr. Polly Wot is describing what she thinks life will be like in the future — in the year two thousand and twenty. **Can you write down what you think she's saying? You'll need a separate piece of paper to write on.**

You could start like this:

In the year 2020 nobody will do any cleaning because robots will do it all.

When you write about things that are going to happen in the future you use the future tense.

We'll get you Sid.

You used the future tense then.

After him!

LAST TRAIN FROM GHOUL END

GHOUL END

TICKETS

WEREWOLF WAY

SPOO

START HERE

RODENT AVENUE

GARGOYLE'S GUESTHOUSE

BONE STREET

HANGMAN'S WA

TOMB STREET

Skulk has just missed the last train from Ghoul End Station..

He drove the long way round because he had to drop off little Willie Spook at school and he did so like the view over the bog from Gallows Hill.

Which way do you think Skulk drove?

Mark it on the map.

What is the shortest way to the station? Write down your instructions for Skulk.

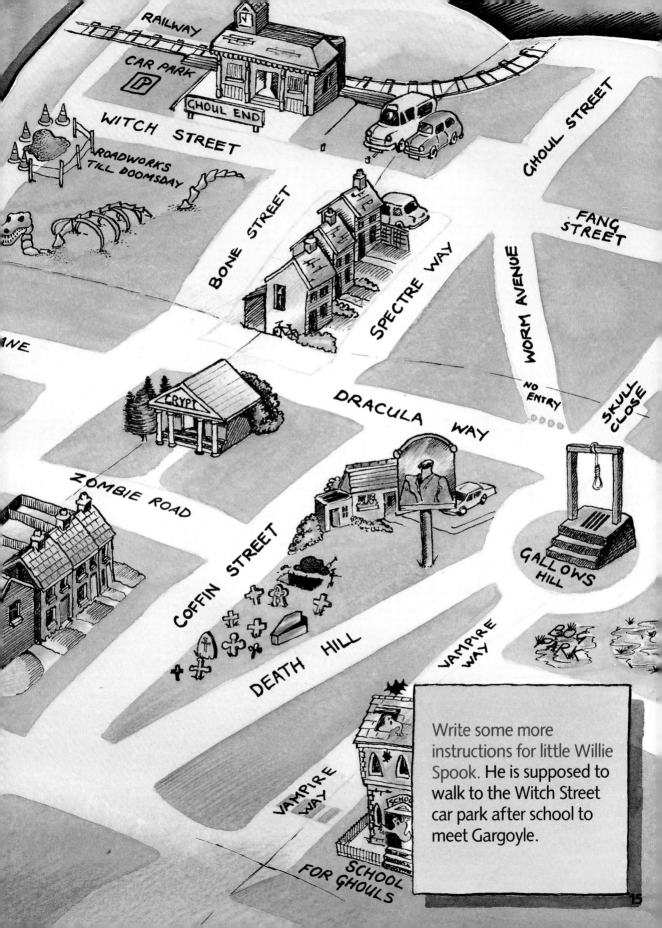

Write some more instructions for little Willie Spook. He is supposed to walk to the Witch Street car park after school to meet Gargoyle.

Sid started straight away. This is what he wrote.

Dracula

The church bell strikes midnight. The wind howls and hisses through the trees. A cloud blots out the moon.

A ghostly castle stands on the hill. Deep down inside a strange creaking is heard, then a CRASH! The sound echoes up the stairs. Dracula is on the prowl!

✓ 10/10
Excellent work Sid!

Oh no! I haven't written anything yet. I'll have to copy what Sid has done.

        ww   **sp**   **sp**

'The lunch bell striks midnite.

    church   strikes midnight

This is what Tatty Tricia's work looked like.

You'll have to be teacher and mark Tricia's terrible work. You could try using the marking guide above. Give her a mark out of ten.

Drackula

the lunch bell striks midnite the wind howels and hisses thoug the knees a clod blot's out the moon. A gostly cake stand's on the till deep down inside a strang creeking is herd then a CRASH! the sand echoes up the stairs. Its dracula on the goal?

17

James Bong's Colour Code

James Bong has to think up a new code.

This one uses three different colours, and a noughts and crosses frame. You draw a frame in each colour. Then you fill them up with letters, like this:

A	B	C
D	E	F
G	H	I

J	K	L
M	N	O
P	Q	R

S	T	U
V	W	X
Y	Z	

James Bong has received a message from his Boss N using this code. What does it say?

Here's a message for you.

James Bong wants to meet you tonight. Send him a message in code saying where and when you will meet him.

Poems that have shapes

There are poems that fit into the shape of the things they are about.
Look at this one about a fish.

see beneath the water swim
darting fishes silent silver tails
flashes swishing
suddenly still in the rustle shade
while the rushes

Can you see what shape this is?

soft

dripping

This looks good, I wish I could eat it!

Here are some words that you could use for the poem that goes into the shape. Choose the ones that you like and add more of your own. We've already put two in for you.

pink	creamy	softer
white	freezing	stickier
cold	warm	soggy
icy	wafer	squishy
melting	crisp	
thawing	sweet	
dripping	hard	
soft	bite	

lurking

danger

swift

What other words could you put in this shark shape?

THE CELLAR

Murphy and Cassie have found a treasure map in an old empty house.

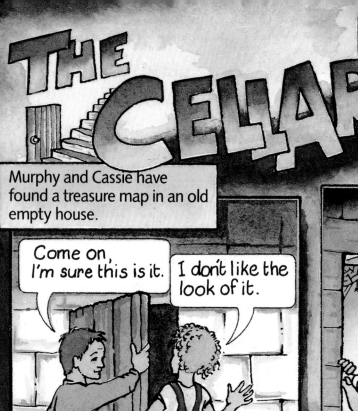

What's all this about then?

I think this is going to be scary

Come on, I'm sure this is it.

I don't like the look of it.

This is where the X is marked.

There's nothing in here.

BANG

It's locked. I can't get it open.

Let me try.

Help! Let us out!

It's no good. This house has been empty for months.

Help me look. There may be another way out.

We'll be trapped for ever!

Quick! Over here. I've found something.

What are all those little marks?

They're speech marks, of course!

See if you can write in what Murphy and Cassie say when the story is written out without pictures.

We've started doing it.

Murphy pushed open the heavy door and shone his torch into the cellar.

"Come on," he called, "I'm sure this is it."

Cassie stood in the doorway. "I don't like the look of it," she said, shivering.

Murphy shone his torch on the map. "_____," he said.

Cassie had begun looking round the cellar. The stone walls were cold and

damp. "_____," she said.

Suddenly there was a loud bang. They both spun round. The door had slammed

shut. Murphy ran to it. He tried to turn the handle.

"_____," he shouted. "_____."

Cassie ran over and tried to help him.

"_____," she said, pushing hard against it.

Murphy began to bang on the door.

"_____," he cried.

Cassie pulled him away. "_____," she said.

"_____."

Murphy put his head in his hands. "_____," he cried.

Cassie took the torch and shone it round the cellar.

"_____," she said. "_____."

Something on the floor glinted in the torch light. It was a large metal

ring, attached to one of the flag stones.

Cassie grabbed hold of it and called to Murphy.

"_____."

Slowly she pulled the ring and the stone lifted . . .

What do you think was under the stone? We've only done a little bit of the last picture. You could finish the picture.
Can Cassie and Murphy find a way out? What dangers will they meet before they are free? Write your own ending for the story.

A TRICKY WORD SEARCH

These are the words to use.

occasion
usually
separate
failure
humorous
conscious
business
library
disappoint
disappear
deceive
receive

You can't even spell easy words right, Trish.

This is a wordsearch for you to make. You can then try it out on somebody else.

The tricky bit is that you will use words which people often spell wrongly. So make sure you spell them right when you write them in.

The letters in red show where people sometimes get the words wrong. So look carefully before you write them in! You'll have to write the letters carefully too. When you've put all the words in, fill up the other squares with any letters you like.

But I orlways spel wurds rite!

Then try it out on somebody. You'll need to give the person a list of the words you have hidden in your wordsearch

Wouldn't you like to do my word-search, Weasel? It's about time you did some work!

I really must go and have a lie down.

 On the next two pages there is a game for you to play. You do not need to pull the pages out to play it. It's about making a film.

Before you play it, you have to finish making it!

The first thing you need to do is to cut out the 12 squares on the edge of this page. They are the actor, camera and script cards. You could stick them onto card if you like.

Look at the board now. You play the game by shaking a dice to move round the board. The **red squares** are where things go wrong.
These might be things like:
- you lose the script
- the leading actress is ill
- bad weather stops filming

Think of other things that might go wrong and write them as neatly as you can in the **red squares** on the board.

In the **green squares** write the things that help you make the film. These might be things like:
- you get the star actor you want
- you get new equipment
- you get the money to pay the extras you need for the crowd scenes

 Find someone to play with and now play the game. You will need a counter or button for each player, and dice.

When you land on one of the corner squares you can collect one of the cards for camera, actor or script. So if you land on the yellow corner square you can collect one of the yellow camera cards. If you land on the blue corner square you can collect one of the blue script cards and if you land on the orange corner square you can collect an orange actor's card. The winner of the game is the first person to collect all three types of card.

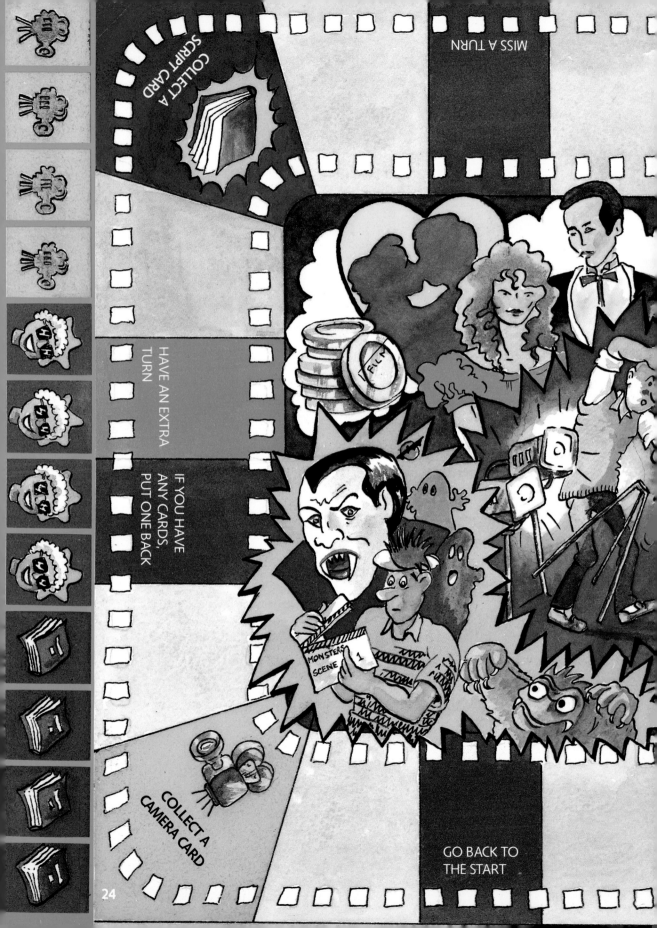

Just imagine that one morning you get:—

a letter from Gargoyle

Gargoyle's Guest Hou...
3 Rodent Avenu...
Ghoul End
Gloomshire
ZK 3 4Bk

Write yesterday's date here.

Write your name here.

Dear

Skulk and I really need a holiday. I'm writing to ask if we can come and stay at your house for a week or two.

We sleep most of the day, so we could use your bed while you're not using it. Please make sure the sheets are nice and damp, though. We won't need any special food either – we can just share your maggoty marmalade and mouldy bread for breakfast. Skulk loves toad in the hole and I like hot dogs. (We'll bring our own toads and dogs.)

I'm sure your family will agree. Just write and let us know when we can come.

Yours sincerely

Gargoyle

P.S. Don't forget to order a couple of extra buckets of slime from the milkman.

What would your family say? They probably won't let Skulk and Gargoyle stay! You have to write back to say no, but you don't want to hurt their feelings. Write Gargoyle a letter, making lots of excuses — you can make them as silly as you like!

No! No! No! No!

Aggagghh!

Or you can pretend that your parents agree. (Perhaps they don't realise what Skulk and Gargoyle are like!) Write a letter making all the arrangements for them. (For example, think of all the things you'll need to buy. . . .)

Write your address here.

Put today's date below it.

Start your letter here with 'Dear Gargoyle'.

Finish off with 'Yours sincerely' and then your name below it.

Edwina's Kitchen

Edwina has an unusual job. Some of the things she keeps in her kitchen tell you what her job is. **List them in the space above the picture and then say what you think her job is.**

Edwina is also very careless. There are many dangerous things happening in her kitchen. For each one there is a line going to a box. **Write what each dangerous thing is in its box.** We've done one for you.

Things to do with Edwina's job

1. _____

2. _____

3. _____

4. _____

I think Edwina is a ....

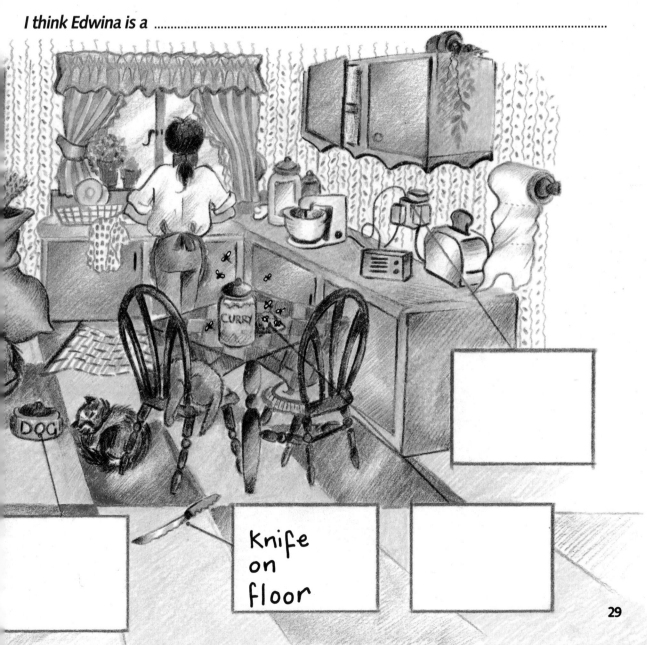

Knife
on
floor

Super Titch

TOP SECRET

...and the disappearing ice-creams!

I was sitting in my office when the phone rang. It was the editor with a new story for me.

> _____ to Brighton immediately and _____ some disappearing ice-creams.

··· Suddenly a thick mist _____ the beach.

It _____ after a few minutes. Everywhere children were _____ and _____ empty ice-cream cones. Something very peculiar was _____ .

I ____ behind an ice-cream kiosk and _____ my glasses.

> This is a job for Super-Titch!

Hatchet _____ on a strange looking machine. It _____ water up from the sea and _____ the beach with a fine mist.

Then he _____ the vacuum hose towards the people. In a few seconds it had _____ up all the ice-cream within range.

> Look everybody! All these words are **verbs.** They tell us what people are doing.

brought	drunk
covered	eating
cried	flew
crying	fly
dived	go
drank	happened

What's this? Those two robbers, Gus and Hatchet, have been at it again!

Read this story and fill in the gaps. Look at the list of words. They are in alphabetical order. There isn't always just one right answer — pick the word you think is best. Don't use any word more than once and be careful — we've put some wrong words in the list which don't fit any of the gaps!

Two hours later I was _____ on Brighton beach. Children were _____ happily and _____ ice-cream.

Whoosh! I _____ into the sky. I could _____ one boat near the shore.

I _____ down onto the deck and _____ through the cabin window. Gus and Hatchet! Two master villains!

Hatchet _____ to a huge vat of ice-cream. A long vacuum hose _____ out of the side.

We need one more lot, Gus!

I quickly _____ the wheel from Gus. "Oh no," _____ Hatchet, "Super Titch!" Gus and Hatchet both _____ over the side.

I _____ the huge ice-cream container to the beach. A few minutes later hundreds of children were happily _____ themselves with the ice-cream.

happening	laying	pointed	sprayed
laid	lifted	removed	stuck
hidden	lying	saw	stuffing
holding	need	see	switched
investigate	peered	seized	sucked
jumped	playing	shrieked	turned

31

THE DISAPPEARING SPELL

I must get this right before the spell competition.. but half the spell has disappeared!!

Whatever shall I do?

Can you write in the missing parts of the spell? Try to think of other things that could go in. Your spell should rhyme but try to make sure that each line names a different object for the spell.

This will make you disappear,
Try it when there's no-one near.

First, you need eleven dogs,
....

Then throw in a lot of ice,
....

Take a lock of human hair,
....

Then add drops of burning gold,
....

Add one purple dragon's scale,
....

Stir it round until it's hot,
Hold your nose and drink the lot.

ces

spices,

little mices,

some rats,

bunch of cats,

effective lotion

around your nose,

and on the toes.

Yuk!

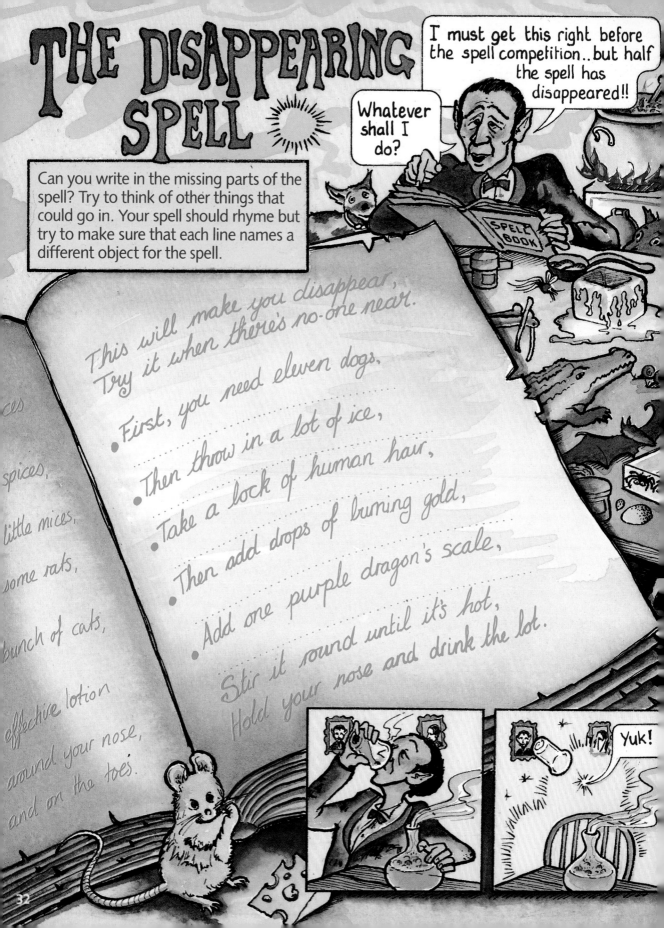

What's in the bag?

The pictures show the contents of Janice and Amy's bags. What do they tell you about Janice and Amy? Which of the statements below the pictures are *probably true* or *probably false*? Write true or false. We've done the first ones for you.

Janice

1. Janice wears eye make-up but not lipstick. ***Probably true***

2. Janice does not have a telephone at home. ***Probably false***

3. Janice shops at the supermarket. ***Probably***

4. Janice has no children. ***Probably***

5. Janice likes reading. ***Probably***

6.

7.

Amy

1. Amy has long hair. ***Probably true***

2. Amy drives a car. ***Probably false***

3. Amy does not wear make-up. ***Probably***

4. Amy does not like football. ***Probably***

5. Amy likes chocolate. ***Probably***

6.

7.

I'll just have a look in mum's bag!

..... and I'll look in Dad's pockets!

In the spaces we've left for you write down at least two more things about Janice and Amy which are *probably true* or *probably false*.

You could collect together some objects which you could pretend you'd found in a person's bag or pocket. Write down what you could say about the owner. Ask someone else to look at the objects and see if he or she writes down the same things.

The amazing chase

Mr. and Mrs. Potts are always having rows. Or rather, Mr. Potts is always being chased by his wife. **Can you complete this amazing chase?** We've finished the first verse for you.

'Come here,' cried Mrs. Potts,

and they were off.

Mr. Potts panted

under the table

into the dining room

through the door

down the path

crashed into the gate

jumped over it and nearly fell

into a puddle.

'Come here,' cried Mrs. Potts,

and she gained on him a little.

Mr. Potts whizzed

across ....

round ....

bounced ....

staggered ....

beside ....

and found himself in front of

....

'Come here,' cried Mrs. Potts,
and she gained on him a little more.
Mr. Potts dashed
past ....
waded through ....
fell into ....
climbed out ....
wriggled round ....
and almost ....

'Come here,' cried Mrs. Potts,
and now she could almost reach him.

Mr. Potts gasped
between ....
slid back ....
fell flat ....
pulled himself out of ....
and wondered ....
before ....

'Gotcha!' cried Mrs. Potts
and Mr. Potts ....

What's this about?

It's a boring title.

Here are three pictures. It could be about any of them.

Here's how you can write an exciting story about the visitor. You'll need a piece of paper.

On the paper, write:

The Visitor

Who are the people?

Where are they?

Why is the visitor there?

How do they feel?

What happens next?

Now choose one of the pictures, and think up answers to the questions.

Just a few words will do.

Here's one we've done as an example. It doesn't have to be neat!

The Visitor.

Who are the people? Tramp. Brother of lady who lives in house. He has been away for ~~30~~ 10 years. He is Edward. She is ~~Susan~~.

Where are they? ~~Susans~~ Susan's house, ~~in Devon~~ Very posh.

Why is visitor there? He's come back from abroad. She kicked him out 10 years ago.

What are they like? She is a snob. He is brave. Kind? Proud ~~but~~ angry with her – he has made lots of money but he dressed up like a tramp on purpose to trick her.

How do they feel? She is shocked to see him. He is

What happens next? She is horrible to him, so he shows her all the ~~money~~ in his parcel and nice clothes etc. too. He says he is going to ~~kick her~~ buy the house and kick her out!

36

Now use what you have written to write your story.

You may want to change the order of the questions, and add other ideas.

Now you can use your ideas to start your story. We've started ours like this.

You can do the same thing when you have to write a story at school! Think of some questions like who? when? where? why? what? how? and write down rough answers to them before you start your story. Ask the teacher first though.

The Visitor

Susan was alone in the big house. She sat by the fire and she was dozing knitting. It was warm by the fire and she was just dozing off when there was a loud knock at the door

How do you want to start your story?

A SPORTING CROSSWORD

Can you do this crossword?

CLUES

Across

1. A game like hockey. (6)
4. It sounds like a fruit drink. (6)
5. Soccer. (8)
8. Racing engines, but not on roads. (10)
9. American rounders. (8)
10. Players use an oval ball. (5)
12. Are you stumped for this clue? (7)
14. Using the power from breaking waves. (10)
19. You need a shuttlecock to play this. (9)
20. This is done with thin swords. (7)
21. Riding, jumping and dressage. (8)
22. You need very smooth grass for this game. (5)
23. Flying with no engine. (7)
29. Players use skates, sticks and a puck. (3,6)
30. A lot of hot air is needed for this. (10)
31. Chasing animals. (7)

Down

2. Girls put the ball through the mesh. (7)
3. This is done on white water. (8)
6. You need a bow and arrows for this. (7)
7. Jumping into mid-air, with support, from aeroplanes. (11)
8. Climbing high natural obstacles. (14)
11. Men put the ball through the mesh. (10)
13. On foot. (7)
15. British baseball. (8)
16. You need clubs for this club. (4)
17. Played at Wimbledon. (6)
18. On horseback. (6)
24. Off the high board. (6)
25. Using wind power on the sea. (7)
26. Exploring caves. (9)
27. Using a two-wheeled vehicle. (7)
28. Travelling on snow. (6)

You'll find the answers on page 46.

POST A POSTER

Would you like to make a poster?
Perhaps you would like to advertise your . . .

FANTASTIC DISCO

MUSIC

refreshments

DANCING

Fabulous

FANCY DRESS

party

RECORD—BREAKING

Athletics Meeting

You can use the opposite page to plan your poster.
Remember that you can use different kinds of lettering, such as:—

lower case & lower case

CAPITALS & **CAPITALS**

THREE-DIMENSIONAL

Multicoloured!

IMPORTANT

Write gently in pencil, in case you need to make any alterations.

Don't forget to come to :—

ON

AT

TICKETS

Whatever it is! Nice big writing here.

Put the day and the date here.

Put the place here.

There is room for some labels e.g. refreshments, or pictures here.

Put the price of the tickets here.

When you are happy with your rough poster, find a large piece of thick paper and do the real one!

James Bong and the hidden microfilm

Agent 002½ (alias James Bong) is just leaving his hotel room to have dinner.

While he is out, his room is searched by two secret agents. They are looking for a hidden microfilm.

James starts writing his notes. He has written down the first difference that he can see. **How many can you spot and write down?**

Notes

1. Book has been turned round.
2. _____
3. _____
4. _____
5. _____
6. _____

7. _____

8. _____

9. _____

10. _____

11. _____

12. _____

Where do you think James Bong had hidden the microfilm? Do you think the enemy has it now?

This story is told in three ways. We have left some yellow gaps. Can you fill them in?

1

Gargoyle and Skulk are going out into the kitchen garden to look for fresh worms and slugs.
Gargoyle gives Skulk the fork.
'Here you are, Skulk.' he says, 'You get the worms. I'll look out for slugs.'
'O.K. Gargoyle,' says Skulk.

Gargoyle begins to pick the slugs off the cabbages.
'Good job it rained last night,' he says.
'There are plenty out today.'
Skulk has started digging. He holds up a long worm.
'Here's a long, fat, juicy one!'

2

(Gargoyle and Skulk are standing on the kitchen steps)

Gargoyle: *(passing Skulk a fork)*
Here you are, Skulk. You get the worms, I'll look out for slugs.
Skulk: O.K. Gargoyle.

(In the garden)

Gargoyle: *(picking up slugs from the cabbages)*
Good job it rained last night. There are plenty out today.
Skulk: *(holding up a worm)*
Here's a long, fat, juicy one!

Here you are, Skulk. You get the worms. I'll look out for slugs.

O.K. Gargoyle.

...n the garden?

You could write a different ending for the story or the play. We have left you a space.

Suddenly Skulk hits something hard in the ground with his fork. He shouts over to Gargoyle.

'   '

But Gargoyle wants to get on with what he is doing.

'   ,' he says grumpily.

Skulk: (waving his fork excitedly)

Gargoyle: (grumpily)

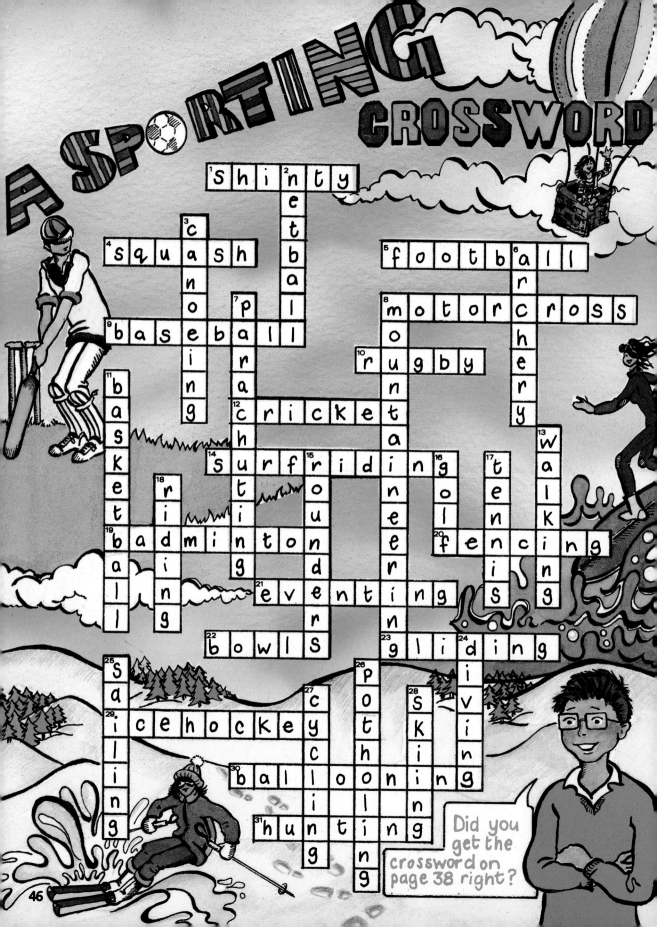

A SPORTING CROSSWORD

Did you get the crossword on page 38 right?

46

the SUCCESS!
AWARDS CEREMONY

Be the judge and give these famous awards to the pages you thought were best. Write in the names of the activities you choose on the lines.

I give the SUPER TITCH ICE-CREAM AWARD to the activity I enjoyed most.

This was ....

I give the JAMES BONG HAT AWARD to the activity I did best.

This was ....

I give the SKULK JUICY WORM AWARD to the activity I thought was the funniest.
This was ....

But I give the ROGER THE ROTTER STINKING DUSTBIN AWARD to the activity I thought was the worst.

This was ....

I didn't like this one because ....

Try to give a reason. Was it really boring? Was it not funny? Was it too hard?

SUCCESS!
means GREAT IDEAS

66 *The very best educational process lies in a confident partnership between child, parents and teachers.* **99**

Success! gives you the chance to make your contribution as effective as possible. We provide a range of imaginative opportunities for you to select from. They can be combined in different ways to achieve the progress you are looking for.

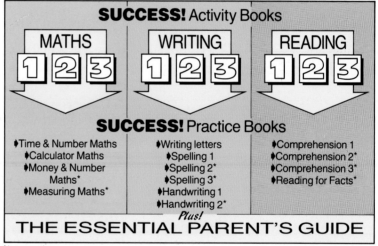

SUCCESS! Activity Books

MATHS 1 2 3   WRITING 1 2 3   READING 1 2 3

SUCCESS! Practice Books

- ◆Time & Number Maths
- ◆Calculator Maths
- ◆Money & Number Maths*
- ◆Measuring Maths*

- ◆Writing letters
- ◆Spelling 1
- ◆Spelling 2*
- ◆Spelling 3*
- ◆Handwriting 1
- ◆Handwriting 2*

- ◆Comprehension 1
- ◆Comprehension 2*
- ◆Comprehension 3*
- ◆Reading for Facts*

Plus!
THE ESSENTIAL PARENT'S GUIDE

* in preparation

SUCCESS! *activity books*

This book is only one of nine activity books covering Maths, Writing and Reading. These books provide challenging and attractive exercises in the *whole business* of the main subjects.

You can choose the subject or subjects that you think particularly need help, and start with the first Level in each one to see how much progress can be made.

SUCCESS! *practice books*

This is a series of books designed to improve specific skills which are part of the whole business of each subject. The exercises are easier than the Activity Books, but they are still lots of fun to do. They concentrate on building ability and confidence in the basic tools everyone needs to be good at the subjects.